Every Dog's Dream Rescue

A portion of all profits earned from your purchase of this book will be sent to Every Dog's Dream Rescue, Inc., a group of compassionate volunteers working around the clock to provide a safe haven for all the animals that are bought into their rescue facility. Every Dog's Dream not only maintains high-quality care for rescued dogs; they also take in cats and small animals. They operate an adoption center located within the Petco facility on Harry L. Drive in Johnson City, New York, where they always have an abundance of cats and kittens and a number of puppies up for adoption. Every Dog's Dream helps families across New York State to care for stray cats. They also help provide food and veterinary care for those who cannot afford to pay but don't want to give up their animals.

To find out more or to donate, go to: EveryDogsDream.org

Caring for Wild Animals

Village Earth Press

Copyright © 2017 by Village Earth Press, a division of Harding House Publishing.

All rights reserved. No part of this publication may be reproduced or transmitted in any form or by any means, electronic or mechanical, including photocopying, recording, taping, or any information storage and retrieval system, without permission from the publisher.

Village Earth Press
Vestal, New York 13850
www.villageearthpress.com

First Printing
9 8 7 6 5 4 3 2 1

ISBN: 978-1-62524-454-3
series ISBN: 978-1-62524-449-9

Author: Rae Simons
Design: Micaela Grace Sanna

Caring for Wild Animals

RAE SIMONS

TABLE OF CONTENTS:

Introduction	10
1. Our Brothers and Sisters	14
2. Wild Animals' Homes	28
3. Wildlife in Trouble	42
4. Wildlife Neighbors	52

Did You Know?

Raccoons are very smart. They are smarter than cats—and almost as smart as monkeys.

Introduction

To parents and teachers:

....

Animal lives matter. Human welfare and animal welfare are interwoven so tightly that they cannot be separated. In other words, what hurts animals will ultimately hurt us as well.

We can see this at the planetary level. As animals lose their habitats because of climate change, pollution, deforestation, and other factors, human well-being is also threatened. Sometimes, people seem to think it's an either-or situation: we either help people (by investing in businesses that are harming the environment) or we help animals (by hindering the success of those same businesses). That's not the way things work on our planet, though. We are all in this together. What puts animals at risk is an equal risk to human well-being.

We are not only linked to animals at the biological and environmental level. We also share many of the same emotions with them—and how we treat animals can't be separated from how we treat each other. Mark Bekoff, an evolutionary biologist, said in an interview with *Forbes* magazine:

> how we treat other animals has direct effects on how we feel about ourselves ...compassion begets compassion.... So, when we're nice to other animals and empathize compassionately with their physical and mental health we're also spreading compassion to other people.

The more scientists learn about animals, the more they find that the creatures with whom we share our planet are far more amazing than we ever knew. Scientists have proven that even fish are conscious and sentient; they've discovered that it's not only our dogs who are sensitive to our pain but that rats, mice, and even chickens are as well; and they also have proof that crows can use tools that are more sophisticated than chimpanzees'. What's more, based on animals' neurochemicals, our furred and feathered friends experience the same feelings of love that humans do.

Earlier cultures thought of animals as our brothers and sisters, but somehow, our culture lost track of that perspective. We need to regain it, not only for animals' sakes but for our own—and we need to teach it to our children. By teaching children how to care for animals (whether pets, farm animals, or wild animals), we are empowering children to become kinder and more responsible.

Psychologists, educators, and other experts agree. The National PTA Congress wrote:

> Children trained to extend justice, kindness, and mercy to animals become more just, kind, and considerate in their relations to each other. Character training along these lines will result in men and women of broader sympathies; more humane, more law abiding, in every respect more valuable citizens.

When children learn compassion and respect for animals, they are better able to extend compassion and respect to each other. A relationship with an animal also helps children gain self-confidence; research even indicates that being with an animal helps children relax and learn better. And by speaking out for those who cannot speak for themselves, children learn leadership and the power of their own voices to make the world a better place.

Village Earth Press has created this series of books because we believe that we need to take action on animals' behalf. We also believe that children should have opportunities to become all they can be. Our hope is that this book will contribute to both those goals.

Read more on this topic (and then discuss with children what you learn). We recommend these books:

The Emotional Lives of Animals
by Mark Bekoff

The Ten Trusts: What We Must Do to Care for the Animals We Love
by Jane Goodall

The Pig Who Sang to the Moon: The Emotional World of Farm Animals
by Jeffrey Moussaieff Masson

The Bond: Our Kinship with Animals, Our Call to Defend Them
by Wayne Pacelle

chapter 1
Our Brothers and Sisters

Pigeons and other birds live in cities. They are wild animals, but they live close to buildings and streets.

We are not alone on our planet. We share the Earth with many, many other living things. Some of these are plants—like grass and flowers and trees—and others are animals. Animals come in all shapes and sizes. They can be tiny, tiny creatures too small to see—or enormous whales that live in the ocean.

Wild animals live in forests and other wild places. They live in places where they can go about their lives without being bothered by humans. They also live in cities, side-by-side with many human beings.

People often enjoy seeing wildlife. Wild animals can be very beautiful. Sometimes, though, people think wildlife is scary. Other times, people think wild animals are pests. Lots of times, people think they have the right to ruin wild animals' homes. They believe humans have more rights than animals. They think people are better than animals.

But guess what? People ARE animals. Human beings are a type

of mammal. Our closest animal cousins are chimpanzees and gorillas. Scientists believe that humans and big apes have a common ancestor who lived millions of years ago.

No one knows exactly HOW life first began on Earth, but scientists believe that there has been some form of living creatures on our planet for more than 3 billion years. The first mammals didn't evolve until about 250 million years ago, though. That's still a long, long time ago!

The first mammals were very tiny, the size of mice. They lived at the same time as dinosaurs. Once all the

What's that mean?

A MAMMAL is an animal that has fur (even if only a very little bit). Mammals also give birth to live babies instead of laying eggs. They feed their babies milk from the mother's body.

An ANCESTOR is someone related to you who lived before you did. Your grandparents, your great-grandparents, and your great-great-grandparents are all your ancestors. Your line of ancestors goes back thousands of years. Without them, you wouldn't be alive today!

To EVOLVE means to change from one thing to another, little by little. Scientists believe this is how all the animals that exist today came into being. They call this EVOLUTION.

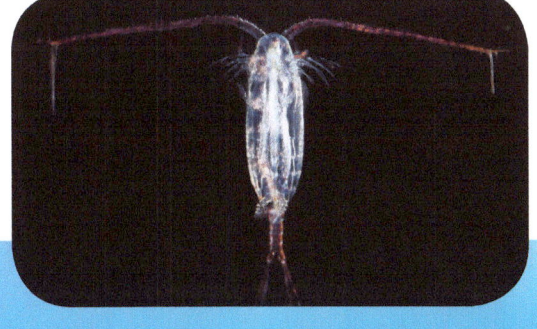

One of these animals is too tiny for you to see unless you looked at it under a microscope. The other one is about the size of a swimming pool—and it weighs as much as a fire engine.

Our Brothers and Sisters • 15

Scientists study fossils like these shown above to learn about the animals that lived on the Earth millions of years ago.

One of the very first mammals may have looked like this.

giant dinosaurs died, mammals had a chance to evolve into larger kinds of animals. All kinds of mammals came into being through evolution.

Here's how it works. A group of animals live in area where most of their food comes from leaves at the top of trees. This means that the animals that have longer necks can reach more leaves. They get more food than the other animals with shorter necks. The long-necked animals are likely to live longer and have more babies. Their babies also have longer necks. Finally, little by little, all the animals in this group have very long necks. We call these animals giraffes!

Other kinds of animals came into being the same way. The animals that

16 • CARING FOR WILD ANIMALS

had something that helped them stay alive were the ones that had babies. Sharp teeth, fast legs, long claws, or hard hooves—these were all things that helped certain animals stay alive while others didn't.

Just like you may have your mother's curly hair or your father's blue eyes, mammal babies looked like their parents. And the ones that were the strongest, fastest, smartest, shyest, or fiercest were the ones that lived to have MORE babies. All kinds of things could help an animal survive. It might be a long tail—a long nose—big ears—or something else altogether. Each kind of animal had something special that helped it live longer and have more babies than the others in its group. This is the way that more and more different kinds of mammals came into being on the Earth.

Millions of years ago, our ancestors' lives weren't so very different from the lives of all the other mammals. People ate plants, they caught small animals and insects to eat, and they **scavenged** for meat left behind by large animals like lions. These long-ago people roamed here and there, looking for food, just like many other animals did. Then, about two million years ago, our ancestors began to make tools and weapons out of wood and stone.

What's that mean?

To SCAVENGE means to find food wherever you can.

Kangaroos evolved in Australia. They don't exist in the wild anywhere else in the world. This baby kangaroo will live completely in a pocket or pouch for the first six months of his life, then slowly start to come out more and more, until around 8 months when he leaves the pocket completely.

Our Brothers and Sisters

Foxes are mammals, the same as people are. Both foxes and people have fur (even though a person's hair is very different from a fox's thick fur). These baby foxes are getting milk from their mother's body.

What's that mean?

The SPIRIT WORLD is a name some people use for a world we can't see or touch, where invisible beings live. Even though we can't see this world, people believe that it touches the world we CAN see. Today, people might call this world "heaven" or the place where God lives.

Compared to many animals, human beings aren't very strong. We don't have sharp teeth or claws like lions and tigers and bears. We can't run fast like deer. We're not as strong as a grizzly bear, and we can't fly like birds or swim as well as fish can. But tools made out of stone and wood made up for humans' weakness. Stone-tipped spears meant people could hunt even very large animals.

Human beings also were smarter than other animals in some ways. People can make plans and come up with new ideas. Gradually, over the years, they made more powerful weapons for killing animals.

At first, people only killed the animals they wanted to eat. Many people still thought of animals as our brothers and sisters. They remembered that we share the same planet with wildlife. They knew that everything on Earth is like one big family. Everyone in the family needs everyone else to get along.

In many places of the world, people thought animals were magic and powerful. They believed that animals were part of the spirit world. They thought that animals brought

Ancient Egyptians believed in a god that looked like a bull. They also worshiped a god named Anubis who looked like a jackal. Hindus believe in a god named Ganesh who looks like an elephant.

What's that mean?

To RESPECT someone or something is to treat them the way you would want them to treat you.

important messages to us from God. Some groups of people believed that animals were like gods. These people worshiped certain kinds of animals. Other people believed that after a person died, she might be born again as an animal—or an animal might die and be born again as a person. Some people believed that animals and people were so close that human beings could sometimes turn into animals. These beliefs about animals were all part of people's religious beliefs. Beliefs like these helped humans **respect** animals. These beliefs reminded people to be kind to animals.

Our Brothers and Sisters   •   19

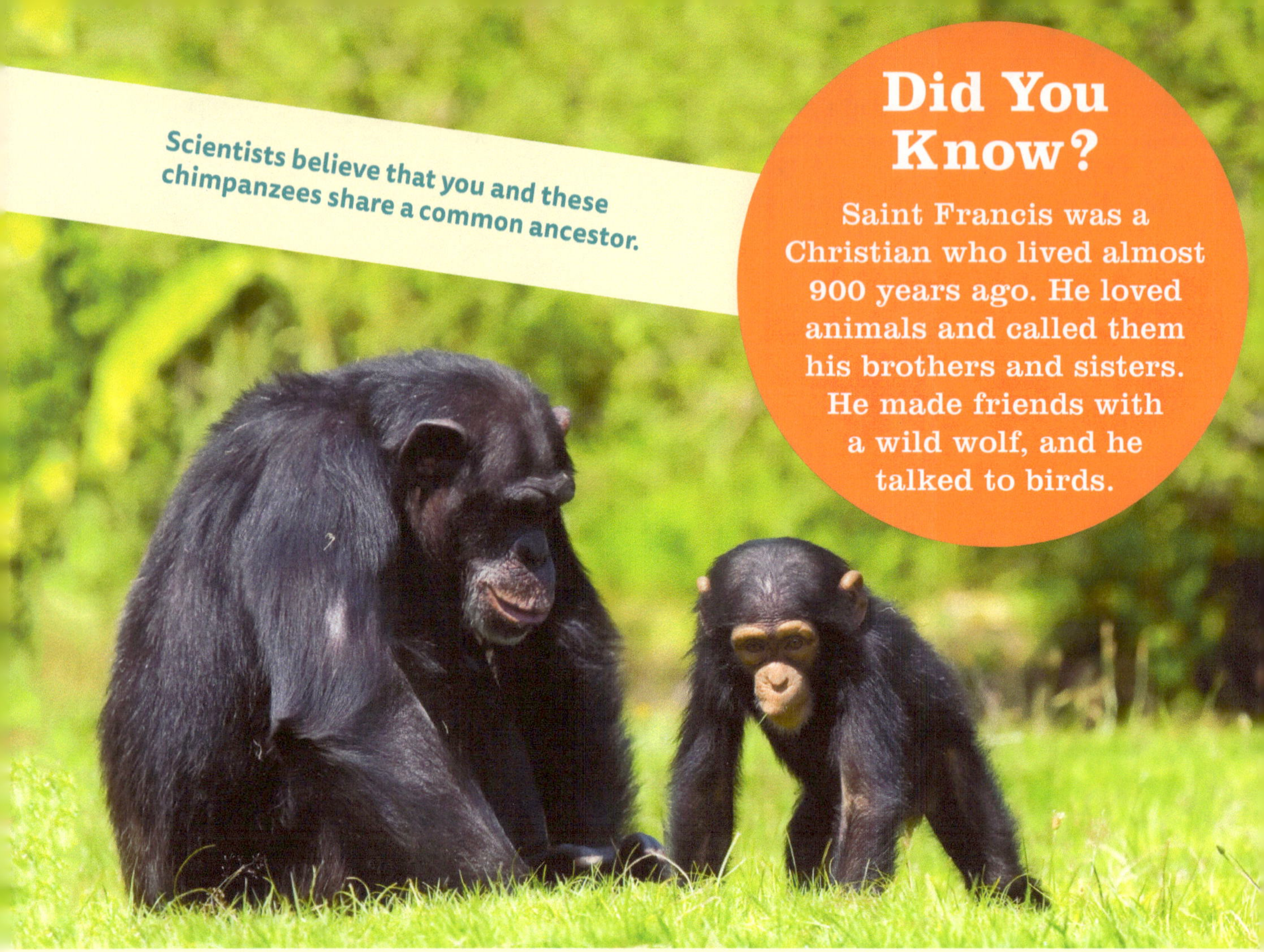

Scientists believe that you and these chimpanzees share a common ancestor.

Did You Know?

Saint Francis was a Christian who lived almost 900 years ago. He loved animals and called them his brothers and sisters. He made friends with a wild wolf, and he talked to birds.

Muhammad—the man who started Islam, the religion of Muslims—loved animals. He especially loved his cat, whose name was Muezza. One day, when it was time for Muhammad to go to prayer, he found Muezza curled up asleep on the sleeve of his prayer robe. Muhammad did not want to disturb her, so he used a pair of scissors to cut off the sleeve. Then he went to his prayers wearing a robe with only one sleeve.

20 • CARING FOR WILD ANIMALS

As the years passed, new religions were born. People began to think about God and the spirit world in new ways. Jews, Christians, and Muslims believed in only one God. They did not believe that animals were gods, and they did not believe that people could become animals. But the leaders of these religions taught that people should be kind to animals. They said that people have a **responsibility** to care for animals.

But as time went by, many people forgot these ideas. They no longer remembered that animals are like our family. Instead, people thought of animals as enemies—or pests. Some animals wanted the same food that people did. Birds might eat all the berries that people wanted, or deer might get in farmers' fields and eat the crops. People began to kill these animals. People also killed the animals they thought were dangerous, like wolves and lions. As people settled down in villages and cities, they drove wild animals away from the places where they had always lived.

Today, humans have killed so much wildlife that some animals have become **extinct**. Others are in danger of becoming extinct.

Wild animals need our help. They need us to treat them with respect. They need us to make sure they have safe places where they can live. Wildlife needs us to pass laws that protect animals from being killed. Most of all, animals need us to take care of our planet, so that the animals will be able to stay alive.

You can make a difference. Wildlife needs YOU!

What's that mean?

A RESPONSIBILITY is something you need to do. The chores you do at home would be one kind of responsibility. Doing your homework would be another.

When an animal becomes EXTINCT, there are no more animals like that alive anywhere in the world. Sometimes animals become extinct because the Earth's climate changes. That's what happened to the dinosaurs. Other times, animals became extinct because people hunted them until they were all killed.

Our Brothers and Sisters

Animals That Are Gone Forever

DINOSAURS:
65 million years ago

WOOLY MAMMOTH:
about 14,000 years ago

SABER-TOOTHED TIGER:
10,000 years ago

IRISH ELK:
about 7,000 years ago

MOA:
about 600 years ago

DODO BIRD:
400 years ago

GREAT AUK:
200 years ago

PASSENGER PIGEON:
100 years ago

CARIBBEAN MONK SEAL:
60 years ago

PYRENEAN IBEX:
15 years ago

Our Brothers and Sisters

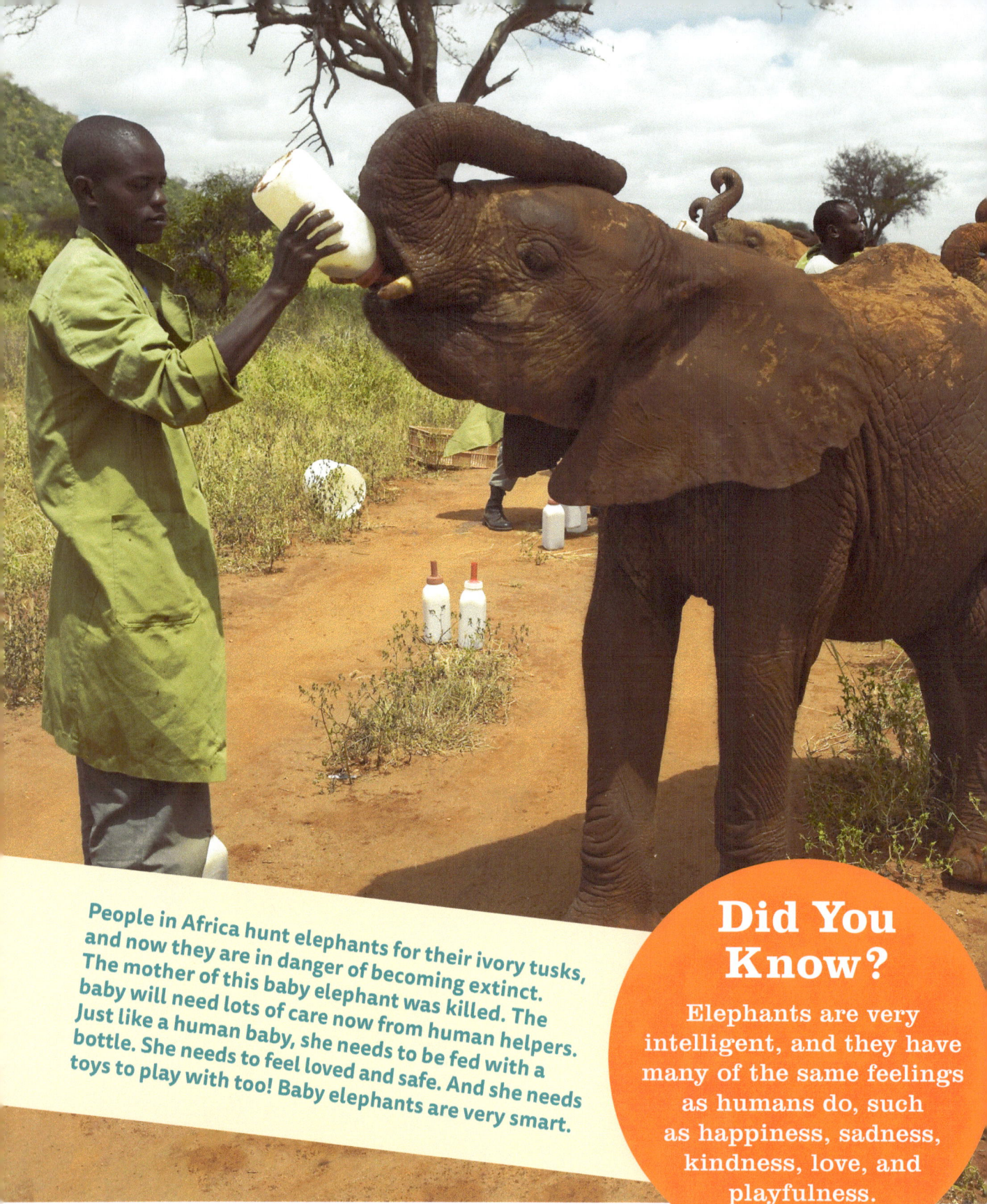

People in Africa hunt elephants for their ivory tusks, and now they are in danger of becoming extinct. The mother of this baby elephant was killed. The baby will need lots of care now from human helpers. Just like a human baby, she needs to be fed with a bottle. She needs to feel loved and safe. And she needs toys to play with too! Baby elephants are very smart.

Did You Know?

Elephants are very intelligent, and they have many of the same feelings as humans do, such as happiness, sadness, kindness, love, and playfulness.

All these animals are in danger of becoming extinct.

Black-Footed Ferret

Blue Whale

Chimpanzee

Giant Panda

Amur Leopard

Orangutan

Indian Elephant

Snow Leopard

Polar Bear

Red Panda

Monarch Butterfly

Arctic Fox

Black Rhino

Leatherback Turtle

Mountain Gorilla

Bengal Tiger

Sea Lion

African Wild Dog

chapter 2

Wild Animals' Homes

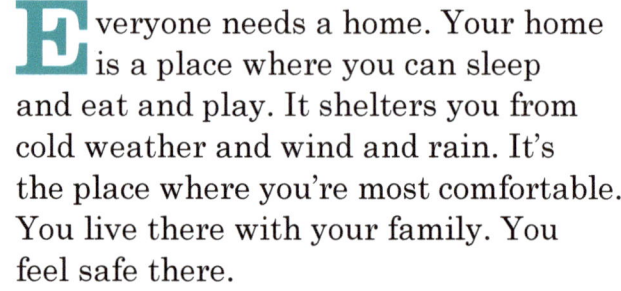

Everyone needs a home. Your home is a place where you can sleep and eat and play. It shelters you from cold weather and wind and rain. It's the place where you're most comfortable. You live there with your family. You feel safe there.

Animals need homes too. When you have a pet, it's your job to give that animal the kind of home it needs. Fish need one kind of home, and birds need another. Farm animals need their own sort of homes. Dogs and cats usually share YOUR home, but they still need you to make sure they have all the things they need to be happy and healthy.

Wild animals have their own homes too. Just like you and your pets, wild animals need a safe place to sleep. They need somewhere they can raise their babies. A bird's home is usually a nest. Most bats use caves for their homes. Many small mammals live in **burrows** in the ground. Beavers build their own homes out of sticks. Frogs live in ponds and swamps. Lots of animals make their homes in trees.

Wild animals also have their own neighborhoods. They're called habitats. These are the special places where wild animals live with other animals and plants. It's where they build their homes. They find food and water there.

Habitats come in different sizes. Habitats can be big like a forest—or they can be as small as a puddle. Some animals roam over a large area. Other animals never go very far from their homes. As long as they can find what they need to be happy and healthy, they will stay in a small area.

Different animals need different habitats. A fish needs clean water. A squirrel needs a place with lots of trees. Bees need a place where flowers grow. Deer need somewhere they have grass and leaves to eat. Each habitat is the right sort of place to give the animals that live there the food and shelter they need.

Lots of different animals and plants will live in the same habitat. That's why it's like a neighborhood. Certain animals and plants live well together.

Think about a pond. If you were to walk around a pond, you would hear frogs plopping into the water. The frogs were hiding in the tall grass, waiting

What's that mean?

A BURROW is a hole in the ground where an animal lives.

Prairie dogs live in burrows in the ground. They pop their heads out to see if it's safe for them to come out.

Wild Animals' Homes • 29

to catch their dinner of flies. When they heard you, they jumped into the water where they feel safer. You might see ducks swimming on the water, and turtles sitting in the sunshine on the pond's bank. Dragonflies would zoom though the air. If you looked at the plants growing around the pond, you might see a snail or a slug clinging to a leaf. Then if you squatted down and looked into the water, you'd see even more animals. Insects called water striders would be zipping around on top of the water. Minnows and salamanders live in ponds. You might also see frog eggs and tadpoles, or a mosquito **larva**. If you were to take some of the pond water home with you, you could look at it with a microscope. Then you'd see even more creatures, tiny little animals too small to see without a microscope.

What's that mean?

A LARVA is a young insect. It usually looks a little like a worm. A caterpillar, for example, is a butterfly larva. When a larva gets older, it turns into an adult insect. A mosquito larva is sometimes called a wiggler, because of the way it moves.

Bats fly around at night, finding bugs to eat, but during the daytime, they go back to their homes to sleep. They like small, dark spaces where they can be safe while they sleep, so they often live in caves. They sleep hanging upside down, with their wings wrapped around them like blankets.

Did You Know?

Wolves usually trot along at about 5 miles per hour—but they can run as fast as 40 miles per hour. That's as fast as a car!

Wolves live in a den, but they need a very large habitat around their home where they can hunt. Their neighborhood usually covers about 50 square miles. Sometimes, when they can't find enough food closer to home, they may roam over as much as 1,000 square miles.

What's that mean?

ALGAE are the tiny plants that live in water. Sometimes, they look like green slime. Ponds need just the right amount of algae. Too much or too little would make the pond unhealthy.

All the plants and animals in a habitat help keep their whole neighborhood healthy. They each have an important job. In a pond, some animals help keep the water clean. Other animals help to spread seeds, so that more plants grow. Some plants and animals are food for other animals. Even the *algae* and the tiny animals too small for you to see are important to the pond's habitat.

Food Chains

The list of who eats what in a habitat is called a food chain. A pond has many food chains that are made up of different plants and animals.

For example, the algae in a pond is at the beginning of a food chain, and a great blue heron is at the end. First, a mosquito larva ate the algae in the pond. The mosquito larva turned into an adult mosquito, and a frog ate it. And then the great blue heron ate the frog. If something happened that killed all the algae in the pond, the food chain would be broken. The mosquito larva, the frog, and the heron would not be able to live there anymore.

Larger animals eat the algae and the tiny creatures. They depend on them for food. Everything in a habitat fits together. They all need each other. If one kind of animal or plant were to disappear, the entire habitat would be upset.

The Earth has many kinds of habitats. Forests, deserts, grasslands, water, and **tundra** are the main habitats in North America.

What's that mean?

TUNDRA is the very cold habitat that is in the far north.

If you were to use a microscope to look at a drop of pond water, you might see something swimming in it that looks like this little guy. ▶

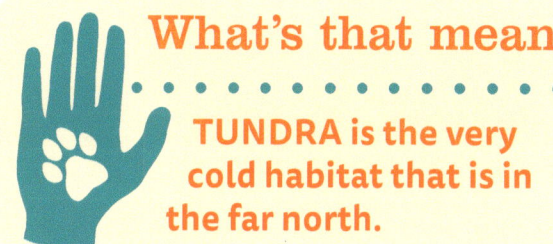

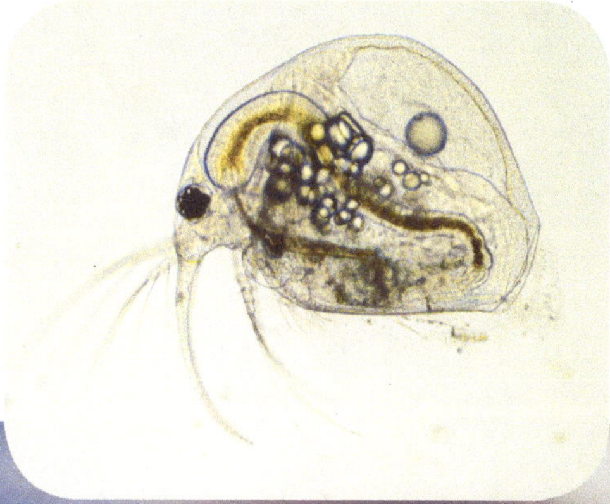

This insect, called a water strider, can walk on water!

These animals live in forest habitats. Some of them live on the forest floor (the ground). Others live in the trees.

Wood Cockroach

Chipmunk

Owl

Raccoon

Deer

Bobcat

You may think that deserts would be too dry for animals and plants to live there. Actually, deserts are full of life. Here are animals that live there.

Scorpion

Horned Toad

Mountain Lion

Roadrunner

Bighorn Sheep

Coyote

Wild Animals' Homes • 35

 Here are some of the animals that live in grassland habitats.

Grasshopper

Burrowing Owl

Prairie Chicken

Badger

Jackrabbit

Pronghorn Antelope

There are different kinds of water habitats. Ponds, streams, and rivers are water habitats. These are some of the animals that live in them.

Beaver

Water Beetle

Crayfish

Catfish

Snapping Turtle

Otter

Wild Animals' Homes

Animals live even in Earth's coldest places. These are tundra animals. They're happy living in cold and snow.

Snowshoe Hare

Snowy Owl

Arctic Fox

Caribou

Polar Bear

White Wolf

CARING FOR WILD ANIMALS

Each of Earth's habitats is different from the others. Some are wet and some are dry. Some are hot and some are cold. The animals who live there like it exactly the way it is. A polar bear could never live in the desert! A raccoon couldn't live in the tundra.

But people are destroying many animals' habitats. When people build houses and roads and stores, they cut down trees. They take land away from animals. Now the animals have to move somewhere else. People also make habitats dirty, so that animals can no longer live there. Cities and factories put pollution into rivers and streams that kills fish and other water animals. The pollution can get in the soil and kill land animals as well.

One of the biggest problems for wild animals' habitats is climate change. People have put so much pollution into the air that it is changing the Earth's climates. The pollution acts like the glass in a greenhouse.

The rainforest is another habitat. Rainforests are in hot, wet places. Toucans live there, and so do many, many other kinds of insects, birds, and mammals. The Earth needs this habitat to be healthy, but people are cutting down many of the rainforests' trees.

What's that mean?

A GREENHOUSE is a special building made for growing plants. The walls are made out of glass. The glass lets in the sun's heat, and then it keeps the heat inside. Plants that would die in the cold can live all winter in a greenhouse.

Did You Know?

Monkeys belong to a group of animals called primates. Gorillas and chimpanzees are also primates. And so are human beings!

The ebony langur is a kind of monkey that lives in rainforests. It eats leaves, fruit, flowers, and insect larvae. Ebony langurs' habitat is being destroyed because people are cutting down the trees where they live.

The pollution holds the heat in and makes the Earth warmer than it used to be. This is dangerous for all Earth's habitats, because their temperatures are changing. Many animals aren't used to living in warmer temperatures.

As habitats change, animals will begin moving into new areas. If desert habitats get larger, for example, desert animals will start moving into places that were once grasslands. The grassland habitat will change. Some animals will be pushed out. Others will die.

Climate change is especially dangerous for tundra habitats. As ice melts, animals like polar bears have nowhere to live. Climate change is killing polar bears.

People made climate change happen. Now people need to figure out how to stop it. They need to stop putting pollution in the air. They need to figure out ways to protect the Earth's habitats.

Wild animals need your help. They need you to speak up so that people will change how they live. You can let people know how important it is to fight climate change. You can tell your family to stop driving cars so much. You and your family can make less trash by recycling and not buying so many things that you don't really need. All those things will help wild animals. Wild animals need you just as much as your pets do!

Here is a book and some websites that will help you learn more about animal habitats:

Habitats: ScienceWorks for Kids
by Evan Moor

Wild Kratts
http://pbskids.org/wildkratts/habitats

National Geographic Habitats
http://environment.nationalgeographic.com/environment/habitats

chapter 3
Wildlife Neighbors

No matter where you live, some kind of wildlife is living nearby. If you live in the country, you see birds and deer, rabbits and woodchucks. If you live in the city, you see pigeons and sparrows, starlings and squirrels. No matter where you live, there are always insects.

Watching wildlife is fun. The more you pay attention to the animals you see, the more you'll learn. If you want to learn even more, every time you see a wild animal, you could use the library and the Internet to find out more. Think of questions—and then search for the answers. For example:

- Why do squirrels chase each other?
- Why do rabbits run in a zigzag when they're scared?
- What's inside a woodchuck's hole?
- How do ants leave a trail so that other ants can follow them?
- How do spiders spin webs?

Wildlife is really interesting! And the more you learn, the more interesting it is.

There are some foods that are safe to feed ducks and other water birds. Shredded leafy green vegetables and grains (like oatmeal or dry barley) are good for these wildlife neighbors.

Lots of people like watching wildlife. People like their wildlife neighbors. They think they're cute, and they want to help them. Sometimes people want to feed wildlife—but this isn't always a good idea. Your pets need you to do what's best for them. Wild animals need you to do that too. Feeding them usually isn't what's best for them.

Reasons Not to Feed Wildlife Neighbors

Most people food isn't good for wild animals. For example, ducks, geese, and swans that eat bread, popcorn, and crackers can get bad health problems. Their wings may not work the way they're supposed to.

Wildlife Neighbors

Feeding wild animals can also make them stop being afraid of people. You might think that would be a good thing. You might like to have wildlife friends that trust you. But not everyone will feel the same way you do. If wild animals go to someone else's door, expecting to be fed, the people who live there could think they're nuisances. They might shoot, trap, or poison the animals.

In Nature, animals are usually spread out. They don't hang out in big groups. When wild animals start gathering around a feeder, if one of them is sick, the others could catch the sickness too.

Things You CAN Do to Help Wildlife

There are some animals that it's okay to feed. If you put birdfeeders in your backyard, you will help birds get food during the winter when food is **scarce**. During the summer, most birds don't need any help finding food. When it's very cold out, though, birds need extra food, to help them stay warm. There are no bugs for them to eat, and seeds and plants may be covered with snow.

Place birdfeeders where their visitors will be safe. Some birds like birdfeeders that are on trees. Others like hanging birdfeeders. A few birds are happiest eating off the ground. Don't put feeders where a cat or another **predator** might catch them! Don't put feeders too near to windows either.

Bears like birdseed too! If you live somewhere that you have bear neighbors, you don't have to worry about them getting into your birdfeeders during the winter. Bears are asleep then. That's another reason why it's a good idea to only feed birds in the winter, and not the summer.

What's that mean?

If something is SCARCE, there's not very much of it.

A PREDATOR is an animal that catches and eats other animals. Hawks, owls, and foxes are all predators. House cats are predators when they catch mice and birds.

Did You Know?

Hummingbirds are the only birds that can fly backward. They can also hover in the air like tiny helicopters.

Most birds don't need you to feed them in the summer—but hummingbirds will be grateful for some extra help finding food. Hummingbird feeders are filled with sweet syrup that gives these tiny birds the energy they need for darting through the air.

Birds may not be able to see the glass. If they try to fly through the window, they could hurt themselves. If you want to place a feeder closer to a window, so you can see the birds better, put decals on the glass so the birds will be able to tell they can't fly through it. If you draw a design on the window with soap, that will work just as well as a decal.

You can buy birdseed at most grocery and department stores. Birds like sunflower seeds. They also like peanut butter and unsalted peanuts. Some birds like suet, which is hard solid fat from a cow.

Don't feed birds most people food. Some people give birds stale bread, but it's not as good for them as birdseed. Don't give birds table scraps either—and NEVER give them chocolate. Chocolate is poisonous to birds, just like it is to your dog.

Wildlife Neighbors

Here are some birds that might visit your feeder:

Nuthatch

Downy Woodpecker

Cardinal

Chickadee

Bluejay

Mourning Dove

Squirrels are clever little thieves when it comes to stealing food from a bird feeder!

Here are some things your family can do to make your yard a good place for your wildlife neighbors:

Give wild animals water. No matter what time of year it is, all wild animals need water (just like your pets do). Even insects need water. Birds also like to take a bath in water.

Plant bushes with berries that birds and other animals can eat.

Leave tall grass growing around the edges of your yard, so rabbits and other animals have a place to hide.

Put a pile of wood or brush in your yard where animals can hide.

Don't put chemicals on your lawn to kill weeds. They can make wildlife and pets sick.

Plant flowers for bees and other insects. The Earth needs bees—but many bees are dying. You can help them by giving them a safe place to live and eat. You don't need to be afraid of them! Bees won't hurt you if you leave them alone.

Put up a bat house in a tree. Bats need safe places to sleep. And they'll return the favor by eating the mosquitoes in your yard.

Wildlife Neighbors   •   49

Leave some dead leaves on your lawn, where bugs can live. Beetles and other insects are good for the Earth—and for your yard. They eat dead plants and animals. That helps dead things turn into soil, where new life can grow.

If you have cats, keep them inside as much as possible. They'll be safer inside—and so will the wildlife in your yard.

Leave puddles or shallow bowls of water for butterflies. A tin pie plate works just as well too.

Make a cool safe place for a toad to hang out. A flowerpot works fine. He'll like it even better if you put a little bit of water in it to help him stay cool.

CARING FOR WILD ANIMALS

Birds aren't the only ones that enjoy birdfeeders. So do squirrels and chipmunks. Squirrels and chipmunks are fun to watch too—but squirrels can quickly eat up all the food and not leave any for the birds. There are special "squirrel-proof" feeders you can use to keep that from happening.

You can also help birds and other wild animals by making your yard a place where animals will be safe and find food. Ask the grown-ups in your family to help you.

If you want more chances to see wildlife, go for a walk in the woods or in a park. Walk quietly, without talking. Or better yet, sit down and don't move at all. Look carefully all around you. At first you might not see anything. But before long, you might notice an ant carrying something on the ground beside you. Then you'll hear a crackly noise, and if you turn your head slowly, you'll see a squirrel scurrying through the leaves. You'll hear a bird calling from a tree. You might see a rabbit or even a deer.

The more time you spend outdoors, paying attention, the more you'll get to know your wildlife neighbors. You'll learn their names. You'll even start to recognize their voices. Each bird has its own call. Squirrels and chipmunks have different sounds they make.

Your wildlife neighbors aren't so different from human neighbors. The more you get to know them, the more you can understand them. You'll enjoy being with them. You'll respect them.

And you'll want to do whatever you can to help them.

chapter 4

Wildlife in Trouble

Have you ever come across baby wild animals? They're very cute! You may wish you could take they home with you. But wild animals aren't meant to be pets.

But what if the baby animal is lost or in trouble? What if it's hurt or sick? What should you do then?

First, you need to be sure the animal really is in trouble. Just because a baby animal is by itself doesn't mean it is lost. Some animals leave their babies alone all day—but the mother always comes back to her babies. If you move them, she might not be able to find them.

What you should do depends on what kind of animal you've found. Different kinds of animals need different kinds of help. Before you try to do anything, always get a grown-up to help you. With a grown-up's help, you may be able to give the baby animal what it needs. If you can't, you should call a wildlife **rehabilitator** for help.

Wildlife rehabilitators know what and how to feed baby animals who are orphans.

Wildlife Rehabilitators

Wildlife rehabilitators are people who have been trained to take care of wild animals that are sick or hurt. Rehabilitators also take care of baby animals whose parents have died.

Rehabilitators don't keep the animals they help. They don't turn the animals into pets. Their job is always to help the animal get better, so that it can return to its home in the wild. If the animal is a baby, they take care of it until the animal can take care of itself.

Each wildlife rehabilitator usually takes care of a certain kind of animal. Some take care of birds. Others take care of small animals like mice and squirrels. Others help injured deer. Wildlife rehabilitators know that each kind of animal needs a different kind of care.

What's that mean?

A REHABILITATOR is someone who helps a sick or hurt person or animal get better. The rehabilitator's job is to get the person or animal back to normal.

Baby Birds

If you find a baby bird hopping on the ground that looks almost like an adult bird, it may be a fledgling. Fledglings are young birds that haven't learned to fly yet. They hop around on the ground for a few days or a week, while they learn. Their parents stay nearby and bring them food.

Keep watch from a distance, and you should see the parents flying down to the young bird once or twice an hour. Keep cats and dogs away until

Wildlife in Trouble

This fledgling is almost as big as its parent, but it still can't fly. Its mother or father will feed it until it is bigger.

These baby rabbits are in their nest in the ground. Don't touch them! Cover up their nest again with a little grass. Their mother will come back to them.

the fledglings have learned to fly. If you watch for an hour or so, and you're sure the parent birds aren't coming back to feed their baby, then you need to get help from a wildlife rehabilitator.

If you find a younger baby bird on the ground, see if you can find the nest. If the baby doesn't seem hurt, you can put it back in the nest. The parents won't care that you touched it, and they will come back as soon as you go away. You can watch from a distance to make sure they do come back.

If the nest has been broken (or if it's too high for a grown-up to reach), you could hang a small basket near to where the nest was. Make sure the basket isn't too deep. The parent birds need to be able to see inside it easily.

Put the baby bird in the new nest and then watch quietly for an hour or so to make sure the parents come back to feed their baby. If they don't come back, then you will need to get help from a wildlife rehabilitator.

If the baby bird is so young that it doesn't have any feathers yet, you shouldn't put it into a basket. Tiny featherless birds need their own nest where they can be warm. You will need to get help right away for the baby.

Baby Rabbits

If you find a baby rabbit that is about as long as your hand and he is able to hop around, he's big enough to be on his own. Baby rabbits are very, very cute—but they do not want to be your

pets! They are happier and healthier being left on their own.

If you find baby rabbits that are too small to hop much, with eyes that are closed and tiny ears, they will usually be in a nest in the ground. Leave them alone. Don't pet them. If you do, the mother will not take care of them anymore.

Even though the babies are all by themselves, they probably have a mother. Mother rabbits only visit their babies once or twice a day. If the nest has been uncovered, cover it up again with a thin layer of grass or leaves. Lay some yarn or string across the nest in a tic-tac-toe pattern.

Come back the next day. If the string has been moved, the mother has come back to her babies during the night. If the string is still there exactly as you left it, call a wildlife rehabilitator.

Baby Squirrels

If you find a little squirrel who has a fluffy tail and can run, jump, and climb, he's probably old enough to be on his own. If you find a squirrel that

This baby squirrel is still too young to survive without his mother. His mother may be nearby, though, waiting to come back to him when you go away.

This fawn is waiting for his mother to come back. He knows to wait quietly until she does.

is so small she has hardly any tail, and she can't move around much, she needs her mother. Leave her where you found her. Give her mother a chance to come back and get her. Keep people and pets away from her, and watch from a little ways away.

If it's cold out or the baby is so young she doesn't have fur, ask a grown-up to put her in a shoebox with a hot water bottle. The grown-up should wear thick gloves, because even young babies can bite. Make sure you put a towel or old cloth between the baby and the bottle, so she doesn't get too hot. Don't cover her with anything. If you do, her mother might not be able to find her. Then wait to see if the mother will come back and get her baby. Don't stay too close, though, or you will scare the mother away.

If the mother doesn't come back for her baby, have a grown-up fill the hot water bottle with hot water again and put it back under the cloth beneath the baby. Then wrap a blanket or towel gently over the baby. Call a wildlife rehabilitator. She will tell you what to do until she can come and get the baby.

Baby Deer

Fawns are left by themselves much of the day. If you find a fawn that is lying down quietly, his mother is somewhere near, even if you can't see her. Leave the fawn alone, unless you know for certain that his mother is dead. Walk away quickly. The mother won't come back until you are gone.

If the fawn is wandering around crying, he probably needs help. Call a wildlife rehabilitator.

Baby Fox

Baby foxes are left alone much of the day while their parents are hunting. They will play like puppies around their den.

If you see baby foxes that look healthy and lively, leave them alone. Watch them from a distance, but don't go too close. If they look sick or weak, call a wildlife rehabilitator.

Baby Opossum

When baby opossums are born, they are about the size of a bee. They will live for about two months inside their mother's pouch. When they get to be about the size of your hand, they come out and start riding around on their mother's back. Mother opossums don't leave their babies alone, but once in a while one will fall off her back without her noticing.

If you find an opossum with a body that is longer than a grown-up's hand

These baby foxes are playing while they wait for their parents. They know not to go far from their den.

Did You Know?

Foxes are related to dogs—but their babies are called kits.

Wildlife in Trouble

This baby opossum is old enough that he's learning to climb. He's still small enough, though, that he needs his mother.

If this baby raccoon's mother doesn't come back for him, he will need the help of a wildlife rehabilitator. Never try to pick up baby raccoons. They have sharp teeth! Raccoons are cute and intelligent—but they are not pets. They belong in the wild.

(don't count the tail), she's probably old enough to be on her own. If she's smaller than that, she probably needs help. Call a wildlife rehabilitator. He will tell you what to do next.

Baby Raccoon

Mother raccoons stay with their babies most of the time—so if you find a baby raccoon by himself, he probably needs help. Put a laundry basket (the kind with holes in the sides) upside down over the baby, with a stone on top so he can't push his way out. When his mother comes back, she will push the basket off him. Since raccoons are nocturnal, she may not come back until nighttime.

If the mother doesn't come back—or if the baby seems sick or hurt—call a wildlife rehabilitator.

Baby Skunk

If you see a baby skunk—or a bunch of baby skunks—running around by themselves, they may be lost. Mother

Baby skunks are as cute as little kittens. You can't take them home, though, and keep them. They belong in the wild. If you find babies without their mother, a wildlife rehabilitator can make sure they get the life they need.

skunks don't like to leave their babies. They have poor eyesight, though, so mothers and their babies sometimes lose each other.

Watch from a distance. If the mother doesn't show up, put a laundry basket over the babies. You may need to ask a grown-up to collect the babies into one spot, so they will fit under the basket. Don't touch them without gloves! Don't put anything on top of the basket. That way, if the mother comes back, she will be able to flip the basket off her babies. If she can't get the basket off by herself, a grown-up could do it for her. If you move very, very slowly around skunks, they may not notice you. If you see a skunk start to stamp her feet, though, move away quickly! If you don't, you could end up very stinky!

If the mother hasn't come back by the next morning, call a wildlife rehabilitator.

Animals That Are Hurt

If you know an animal is hurt, you need to call a wildlife rehabilitator. If you can't find one on the Internet, call an animal shelter or a veterinarian. They should be able to tell you the right person to call. Once you talk to a rehabilitator, she will be able to tell you exactly what to do next.

If the rehabilitator wants you to bring the animal to her, she will tell you the best way to do that. In the meantime, don't try to feed the animal or give it something to eat. It doesn't need either food or water right away—and you could hurt it more by trying to get it to eat. Talk very softly around the animal, and don't make any loud noises. Put the animal somewhere warm and dark. You may want to comfort the animal, but this animal is not your cat or dog. The sound of

Some wildlife rehabilitators are specially trained to take care of birds like owls and hawks. If the bird is injured, the rehabilitator will take care of it until it is well enough to go back into the wild.

your voice will only scare her more—and the more scared she is, the harder it will be for her to heal. Get the animal to the rehabilitator as soon as you can.

Taking Care of Animals

Animals need our help in lots of ways. If you love animals, when you grow up you might want to become a wildlife rehabilitator—or a veterinarian—or an animal trainer. You might want to work in a wildlife **sanctuary**—or be a **zoologist**.

But you don't have to have a special job to take care of animals, and you don't have to wait until you grow up. You can start right now by taking good care of your pets—by working to save wild animals' habitats—and by doing whatever you can to make sure wildlife is safe.

We share our planet with animals. We are like one family, and they are our brothers and sisters. We need them. Without animals, our lives would be sad and boring. Without animals, we would not even be alive!

And animals need us too. They need us to speak up for them and stop people from hurting them. They need us to respect them and care for them.

Animals need YOU!

What's that mean?

A SANCTUARY is a safe place. A wildlife sanctuary is a place where wildlife that has been hurt or abused are taken care of. The animals are safe there.

A ZOOLOGIST is a scientist who studies animals.

Here are some books and a website that will help you learn more about wildlife:

The Nature Connection: An Outdoor Workbook for Kids & Families
by Clare Walker Leslie

Kids' Outdoor Adventure Book: 448 Great Things to Do in Nature
by Stacy Tornio and Ken Keffer

National Geographic Kids
http://kids.nationalgeographic.com/animals/

Image Credits

Cover: Jdgrant (Dreamstime), Jeanninebryan (Dreamstime), Jeffrey Van Daele (Dreamstime), Johannes Gerhardus Swanepoel (Dreamstime), Johannes Oehl (Shutterstock), Moose Henderson (Dreamstime)

Pages 1-4: Alain (Dreamstime), Annilein (Dreamstime), Brian Lasenby (Dreamstime), Denise Kappa (Dreamstime), Elena Elisseeva (Dreamstime), Enrique Gomez (Dreamstime), Jdgrant (Dreamstime), Jeanninebryan (Dreamstime), Jeffrey Van Daele (Dreamstime), Joseph Gough (Dreamstime), Juanita Shore (Dreamstime), Larry Keller (Dreamstime), Micaela Grace Sanna, Mikael Males (Dreamstime), Moose Henderson (Dreamstime), Naluphoto (Dreamstime), Romano Petešic (Dreamstime), Tatiana Morozova (Dreamstime), Twildlife (Dreamstime), Viorel Dudau (Dreamstime), Yanik Chauvin (Dreamstime)

Introduction: Johannes Oehl (Shutterstock), Karl Umbriaco (Dreamstime)

Chapter 1: Alanjeffery (Dreamstime), Americanspirit (Dreamstime), Anna Kucherova (Dreamstime), Artur Maltsau (Dreamstime), Burnel1 (Dreamstime), Chaoss (Dreamstime), Darryl Brooks (Dreamstime), Ekays (Dreamstime), Eric Isselee (Shutterstock), Ethan Daniels (Dreamstime), Gilles Malo (Dreamstime), Grzegorz Gust (Dreamstime), Heinrich Harder, Hoatzinexp (Dreamstime), Jezbennett (Dreamstime), Johan Lamprecht (Dreamstime), Julian Skeels (Dreamstime), Justinhoffmanoutdoors (Dreamstime), Katyamaximenko (Dreamstime), Kristof Degreef (Dreamstime), Linda Bucklin (Dreamstime), Liumangtiger (Dreamstime), Lola Pidluskaya (Dreamstime), Lorraine Swanson (Dreamstime), Mershon (Dreamstime), Micaela Grace Sanna, Monkeyparty420 (Dreamstime), Mr1805 (Dreamstime), Nilanjan Bhattacharya (Dreamstime), Rgbe (Dreamstime), Sanjeev Kumar (Dreamstime), Steffen Foerster (Dreamstime), Taco Gooiker (Dreamstime), Tom Linster (Dreamstime), Valentyna Chukhlyebova (Dreamstime)

Chapter 2: Adrian Ciurea (Dreamstime), Andrew Sabai (Dreamstime), Andylid (Dreamstime), Boaz Yunior Wibowo (Dreamstime), Brian Kushner (Dreamstime), Christopher Elwell (Dreamstime), Copora (Dreamstime), David Burke (Dreamstime), Derrick Neill (Dreamstime), Eric Isselee (Shutterstock), Handsomepictures (Dreamstime), Howard Sandler (Dreamstime), Ivan Kmit (Dreamstime), Janmiko1 (Dreamstime), Jean-edouard Rozey (Dreamstime), Josefpittner (Dreamstime), Kojihirano (Dreamstime), Les Palenik (Dreamstime), Lukas Blazek (Dreamstime), Lukas Blazek (Dreamstime), Martin Kubík (Dreamstime), Melinda Fawver (Dreamstime), Micaela Grace Sanna, Mikael Males (Dreamstime), Miroslav Hlavko (Dreamstime), Moose Henderson (Dreamstime), Nico Smit (Dreamstime), Orval Nelson (Dreamstime), Oseland (Dreamstime), Petar Zigich (Dreamstime), Photosbyjam (Dreamstime), Qliebin (Dreamstime), Rod Kriminger (Dreamstime), Scosens (Dreamstime), Seread (Dreamstime), Sergey Uryadnikov (Dreamstime), Shriram Patki (Dreamstime), Stanislav Duben (Dreamstime), Sumikophoto (Dreamstime), Viter8 (Dreamstime)

Chapter 3: Anjajuli (Dreamstime), Beyondsupermom3 (Dreamstime), Carol Kelpin (Dreamstime), Clearvista (Dreamstime), Colt400 (Dreamstime), Dave Nelson (Dreamstime), Helgidinson (Dreamstime), Judy Kennamer (Dreamstime), Karl Ander Adami (Dreamstime), Lizgiv (Dreamstime), Maria Dryfhout (Dreamstime), Micaela Grace Sanna, Mikelane45 (Dreamstime), Nicola Gordon (Dreamstime), Operative401 (Dreamstime), Paul Sanna, Rebecca Dewstow (Dreamstime), Rkpimages (Dreamstime), Sonya Etchison (Dreamstime), Sue Feldberg (Dreamstime), Susan Sheldon (Dreamstime), Suzanne Tucker (Dreamstime), Tina Patterson (Dreamstime), Trevor Jones (Dreamstime), Wonderwolf (Dreamstime)

Chapter 4: Bruce Macqueen (Dreamstime), Countrymama (Dreamstime), Elena Elisseeva (Dreamstime), Eric Isselee (Shutterstock), Jason Ondreicka (Dreamstime), Karin59 (Dreamstime), Ken Vangorder (Dreamstime), Leslie Banks (Dreamstime), Lynn Bystrom (Dreamstime), Micaela Grace Sanna, Nagylali (Dreamstime), Outdoorsman (Dreamstime), Pixworld (Dreamstime), Pleprakaymas (Dreamstime)

Pages 63-66: Anke Van Wyk (Dreamstime), Brandon Seidel (Dreamstime), Bruce Macqueen (Dreamstime), Christophe D. (Dreamstime), Csaba Vanyi (Dreamstime), Dave Massey (Dreamstime), Federico Donatini (Dreamstime), Gale Verhague (Dreamstime), Gilles Malo (Dreamstime), Hanhanpeggy (Dreamstime), Hdanne (Dreamstime), Johan Lamprecht (Dreamstime), Johannes Gerhardus Swanepoel (Dreamstime), Kclarksphotography (Dreamstime), Kheng Ho Toh (Dreamstime), Kutt Niinepuu (Dreamstime), Lukas Blazek (Dreamstime), Micaela Grace Sanna, Miroslav Hlavko (Dreamstime), Naluphoto (Dreamstime), Paula Masterson (Dreamstime), Rudmer Zwerver (Dreamstime), Solarseven (Dreamstime), Sue Feldberg (Dreamstime)